Playing with Penguins

and Other Adventures in Antarctica

written and photographed by ANN McGOVERN

additional photos by COLIN MONTEATH

Scholastic Inc.

New York Toronto London Auckland Sydney

To Mike McDowell, who made this Antarctic journey possible.

To Frontier Cruises and Salen Lindblad.

To Captain Aye and his wonderful crew.

To Dennis Puleston, Alan Gurney, Vincent Serventy, Peter Carey,
Steve Dawson, Barbara Todd, Roger Sutherland, and Mike Dunn, who shared
their vast knowledge.

To Carys Monteath for being such a lovely, willing model.

To the other Monteaths—Daniel, Betty, and especially Colin Monteath. Colin's
pictures of the huskies, diving Adélies, killer whales, leopard
seals, chinstrap penguin family, and ice halo filled in my spaces. He can be
contacted at Hedgehog House, P.O. Box 33-152, 7A Gwynfa Avenue,
Cathmere, Christchurch, New Zealand.

To Dr. Tetsuya Torii for his photograph of the aurora australis.

ISBN 0-590-44175-2

12 11 10 9 8 7 6 5 4 3 2 1   4 5 6 7 8 9/9

Printed in the U.S.A.   08

First Scholastic printing, November 1994

For Marty Scheiner, who lives in the pages of this book.
His great courage in the last year of his life
made our journey to Antarctica possible.
He loved the wild ice for its
purity, science, and magnificence.
Honoring his spirit, the ice
will forever glow in my memory.

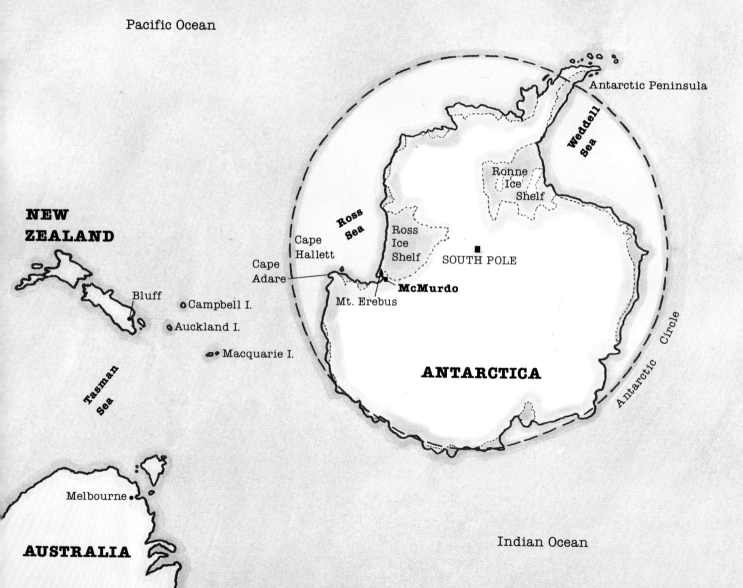

SOUTH AMERICA

Chile

Punta Arenas

Pacific Ocean

Antarctic Peninsula

Weddell Sea

Ronne Ice Shelf

Ross Sea

SOUTH POLE

NEW ZEALAND

Cape Hallett

Ross Ice Shelf

Cape Adare

McMurdo

Bluff

Campbell I.

Mt. Erebus

Auckland I.

Macquarie I.

ANTARCTICA

Antarctic Circle

Tasman Sea

Melbourne

AUSTRALIA

Indian Ocean

March 3

Dear Diary,

I'm sailing to the white bottom of the world and I'm still having trouble spelling it. It's ANTARCTICA, with two *c*'s. Instead of ANT-arctica, I think it should be called ICE-arctica. No ants can live in such a cold, icy place.

Everywhere I look I see ice. On the dark sea, I see icebergs tinted green or blue. On land, I see white, white glaciers and towering frozen mountains.

The _Frontier Spirit_ has seven decks.

Grandma invited me to go with her to Antarctica. We're sharing a cabin on the modern ship, the _Frontier Spirit_. I told Grandma I was starting to keep a diary of my adventures. She said she'll keep a diary of facts for me. I'll put her pages at the end of my diary. Here's the symbol to show that there's more information in Grandma's diary. ❄️

Grandma says Antarctica is the world's coldest, windiest, driest, and highest continent. It's not cold inside the ship. But when I go out on the deck — _brrr_. ❄️

Our cabin is warm and cozy. My bed is on the window side and right now the window is all frosted over from bursts of icy sea spray.

Captain Aye has made 62 expeditions to Antarctica.

The captain makes announcements from the bridge from time to time. We hear his voice booming over the ship's intercom. He just said that the wind is blowing sixty miles per hour. It's force ten. Worse than a gale! No wonder the ship is rolling and heaving. The temperature is one degree below zero Fahrenheit. Summer is over. Antarctic summer lasts only about eight weeks. I wonder how much colder it will get. ❄

The captain's name is Captain Aye. I like to say "Aye, Aye, Captain Aye," but I don't do it in front of him.

There's a lot of complicated equipment on the bridge. The bridge is where the captain and his crew navigate. It's where I watch for whales and icebergs and penguins and seals. It's my favorite place on the ship.

Some icebergs are as big as houses.

We left from New Zealand. We've been sailing for five days and we've been through four storms. Most everyone is seasick, including poor Grandma. But not me. Grandma says I'm a true sailor.

Excuse me, Dear Diary, for not starting to write sooner. But I was so busy exploring this big ship and meeting some of the ninety passengers, the lecturers, the crew, and Mike, the expedition leader. Everyone is very nice to me.

Many different kinds of penguins live in this part of the world, but so far I haven't seen any penguins at all. I've seen plenty of icebergs. And birds with wonderful names like wandering albatross and spotted shag and white-chinned petrel. ❄

The weather changes minute by minute. Today we started out with bright blue skies. Suddenly it turned gray. Then heavy fog rolled in. Then a howling gale blew up. Tonight we might have a gorgeous sunset.

Every day there's been a different lecture about Antarctica — exciting stories of the early explorers and slide shows about the wildlife.

Speaking of wildlife, I can't wait to see some penguins!

I love to see an Antarctic sunset.

March 4

Dear Diary,

I'm scared. We're in the middle of a giant storm and the ship is rocking and rolling! I can hardly write straight. At six A.M., cold ice woke me up! The ice bucket flew from my bedside table and landed right in my bed! Melting ice was all over me and the sheets! Grandma fell out of *her* bed! She was more surprised than hurt. Everything that wasn't fastened down came crashing down — cameras, books, hairbrushes — everything!

The seas are like mountains. Waves are breaking over the ship! Captain Aye just made an announcement from the bridge. The wind is force twelve. About as stormy as it gets! Breakfast will be brought to us in our cabins. We can't leave our cabins till the captain tells us it's safe.

9 A.M.

Breakfast came on paper plates and I ate Grandma's, too. Poor Grandma. She's too seasick to eat. This is no fun. I feel like I'm a prisoner on a ship in Antarctica.

11:30 in the morning

The captain just announced that it's okay to leave our cabins. The ship is still rocking and the seas are very high! It's kind of exciting and I'm not scared anymore. The bridge is closed to all passengers so I can't ask the captain when everything will be calm again.

After lunch

All along the rails in the halls are throw-up bags. I'm glad I didn't have to use one.

Grandma is still in bed, still seasick. The dining room was half empty. I went to lunch by myself. Lunch was sandwiches on paper plates. The chairs were tied down to the floor by chains. From the kitchen I could hear glasses breaking and dishes crashing as they came flying off the shelves.

Mike, the expedition leader, sat at my table and talked about winds that are called the Roaring Forties and the Furious Fifties. ❄ He told me how the *Frontier Spirit* can handle ice. Her hull is ice-strengthened so it can push right through most ice.

I love the names of the different kinds of ice down here: There's green ice, blue ice, grease ice, pancake ice, lily-pad ice, bullet ice, brash ice, ice dust, ice flowers, ice saddles, bergy bits — to name a few.

But if we run into very thick pack ice, we're in trouble. Then only an icebreaker can get through.

I asked Mike if there might be pack ice ahead. You know what he said, Dear Diary? "Probably. Winter's almost here and in Antarctica anything is possible."

Now I'm worried. Will we get stuck in pack ice and have to spend the whole dark winter here?

The *Frontier Spirit* can push through most kinds of ice.

Later

I saw my first penguins!! After lunch, the bridge was open so I went out. Close under the bow of the ship were four royal penguins in the water. I forgot to bring my camera, and the penguins swam away before I could get a picture. Too bad!

It's hard to think of penguins as birds that don't fly. I know they're birds because they have feathers and in the water they do look like sea birds. I want to see them on land, toddling around and looking like waiters in tuxedos.

I'm seeing land — a chain of islands. But it's still not calm enough to lower the rubber boats called zodiacs. I can't wait to ride in a zodiac and get to land and walk among the penguins. When am I going to do that?

Later

Brr. Outside I felt the air growing colder. Mike said we just passed the Antarctic Convergence, when the warm waters of the world's oceans meet the cold Antarctic waters.

You should see all the layers of winter underwear I have on!

A penguin statue and a pair of snow penguins will have to do until we get to see some real ones.

March 5

Dear Diary,

This morning the captain made another terrible announcement. He said we can't land today. We lost many hours last night due to snowfall and poor visibility. Again I'll miss seeing penguins!

Mike is trying to make the best of it. There's going to be a snowman-building party on deck seven.

Much later

Before I went to bed, I visited the bridge. The ship's powerful searchlights were on. The captain looked very serious. He said pack ice was beginning to form.

The captain and the crew are keeping a very careful watch. It was so stormy I stayed inside on the bridge to help them look for ice called growlers. The ship's radar cannot pick up growlers. ❄

I must have fallen asleep in the chair on the bridge because the next thing I knew, Grandma was tucking me into my bed.

You can see why they call this pancake ice.

March 6

Dear Diary,
    Land at last! Today makes up for all the stormy days at sea. It's blue-sky beautiful and so calm. I see lots of icebergs and white mountains all around. The sea is covered with round pancake ice.

Each zodiac holds about twelve people.

Later

After lunch, we anchored off Cape Evans. I took my first zodiac ride to shore. I was glad I was wearing winter underwear, tons of sweaters, and two pairs of socks and mittens.

We went inside a wooden hut that was built in 1911 by the brave explorer Robert Scott and his companions. It's so hard for me to imagine the dangers they faced every day. Everything they used is still here — dishes, cans of food, clothing. Stuff from their scientific experiments is on the worktables. And I saw pony snowshoes. Scott used them on his ponies when he made his brave race to the South Pole. ❄

Scientific equipment from 1911 is still on the table in the Scott hut.

Grandma took a picture of me with some friendly Adélie penguins.

Dear Diary, I saved the best news for last. I finally saw my first penguins on land! Whoopee! On the slopes behind the hut were some adorable little Adélie penguins. And guess what? They *do* look like waiters waddling around in tuxedos.

Then I spent about an hour watching a single emperor penguin, the largest of the penguins. It was almost four feet. About as tall as me. It didn't seem to mind everybody clicking their cameras at it. ❆

"Tobogganing" is a fast way for penguins to travel through the snow. An emperor penguin shows how it's done.

16

Later

I hated to leave the emperor penguin but even with two pairs of mittens on, my hands were beginning to freeze. I warmed up fast back on the ship. It was five degrees below zero out there today. The scenery was so exciting that I bundled up again and went out on deck, watching the ice pancakes and the glorious mountain scenery.

But it's scary. When the weather gets colder, the pancake ice gets thicker. It sticks to other pancake ice and before you know it, it becomes pack ice. And, Dear Diary, you know how I feel about pack ice!

When a whale spouts, it breathes out the warm air in its lungs through its blowhole.

March 7

Dear Diary,

We've gone farther south than any cruise ship has ever gone before! From here it's 726 miles to the South Pole.

Today we had a tour of the ship. It was built to protect the environment. I saw containers to recycle paper, glass, and cans. Kitchen garbage is stowed in cold rooms till the ship returns to port. They even have a machine that prevents accidental oil spills. Grandma says if all ships were like the *Frontier Spirit*, there'd be no problem with pollution from ships.

After lunch

Killer whales were sighted. But by the time I got into my warm clothes, all but one of the orcas had swum away. I could see it spouting. Mike says two hundred thousand orcas live in the Southern Ocean. They feed mostly on seals and penguins. I told Mike that if they eat penguins, I don't want to have anything to do with them. Mike told me I was being silly. He said all creatures eat and in turn are eaten. Everything in nature has a purpose.

McMurdo Base is so huge, it even has a bowling alley.

March 8

Dear Diary,

Today we visited McMurdo, the American base. Ninety men and women stay through the cold, dark winter. ❄

A woman named Betty showed me around. She has golf clubs in her room. They play golf on the ice in their spare time. Inside one of the buildings, I saw tons of up-to-date computerized science equipment.

Betty said that until a few years ago there was a team of sledge dogs at the nearby New Zealand base. Then laws were passed that made them stop using the dogs. ❄

After weeks of feeling so close to nature, I hated to see man-made stuff on the snow. Like buildings and tractors and trucks.

I was glad to get back to nature — to icebergs, to pure snowy mountains — and to penguins!

Later

After lunch, we rode the zodiacs to shore. A wet landing. I'm glad my boots come up to my knees! I explored Discovery Hut, another early hut built by Scott. Everything was almost one hundred years old! Even penguin eggs! And slabs of seal meat that the explorers and their dogs had used as food! I touched the seal blubber. It was still sticky!

In back of Discovery Hut, there was a Weddell seal I wanted to take a picture of. I forgot how slippery the ice was under the snow. Down I went. And there we were — me and the seal — looking at each other lying on the snow!

Click! I got his picture. ❆

Greenpeace Base looks tiny compared with McMurdo.

Later

We picked up a new passenger. She's Pippa from Greenpeace Base. Our ship will take her back to New Zealand. Three others will winter over at the base.

Pippa told me how Greenpeace tries to protect the creatures of Antarctica. I love her story of how Greenpeace saved whales from being hunted. Whalers had moved their boats close to the whales to harpoon them. Greenpeace people followed them. They moved their rubber zodiacs between the whales and the harpooners. The harpooners couldn't shoot their harpoons. They were afraid they'd hit Greenpeace people instead of whales! Greenpeace stayed until the whalers finally went away! Hurrah for Greenpeace!

March 9

Dear Diary,

Good-bye, good weather. It's a blizzard out there today. Sheets of snow are blowing off the great cliffs of the Ross Ice Shelf. The ice shelf is about the size of France. Grandma says it's one of the most amazing natural wonders of the world.

I didn't win the Ross Ice Shelf contest. We were supposed to guess how high it is. I wrote down sixty feet. I wasn't even close. It's over one hundred feet high.

Later

The weather is getting worse. We're supposed to explore Franklin Island this afternoon. Mike said there's a great penguin rookery there.

Mike and another crew member are getting ready to scout the shore. Before we can think about making a landing, there's always a zodiac scouting expedition to see if it's safe for passengers. Sometimes Mike decides that the waves along the beach are too high. Or the shore is too icy for us to land.

When I saw Mike all bundled up and wearing his life jacket, I asked him to take me along. He gave me a look. There's probably a rule about taking passengers, especially kids, on a zodiac scouting expedition. Now he's mad at me. Why didn't I keep my big mouth shut!

Later

The worst thing in the world happened. I'll try to write it down, Dear Diary. But I'm really upset about it.

Thirteen minutes in the cold, cold water — but the men are safe!

About ten minutes after I asked Mike to take me along, I heard the captain's voice on the intercom: "Man overboard! Clear the bridge!" His words sent shivers through me.

I ran down the stairs to deck six. By now, most of the passengers, including Grandma, had heard the captain. Everyone rushed out on deck. People were screaming.

It was Mike and another staff member who fell into the icy waters when their zodiac tipped over! I leaned over the rail and tried to see them. The snow was blowing hard and the wind was whipping the waves into mountains.

A rescue zodiac was lowered into the stormy sea. It seemed forever before the zodiac returned with the men. They were shivering with cold, but they were alive!

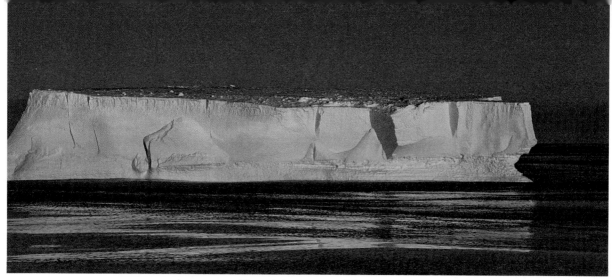

Great towers of ice!

Later, way past my bedtime

At dinner, we talked about why the accident happened. The hook that connected the zodiac line to the ship had frozen! The zodiac couldn't get free. Then a high swell tipped the zodiac and spilled the men into the sea.

Everyone said it was a miracle that they survived. Thank goodness they were all wearing their life preservers. We have to wear them, too, whenever we go into the zodiac.

The captain announced that the men were okay except for tingling fingers and toes. They would be in the lounge later to talk with us.

In the lounge, the captain thanked the doctors and the rescuers who hauled the men to safety.

"In my thirty-five Antarctica trips, I've never fallen into the water," Mike said. "Believe me, you can never take Antarctica for granted."

Later Mike came over to me and laughed, "Still want to come scouting with me?" I guess he's not mad at me after all. I'm so glad he's safe! Just think! If he had taken me along, I'd have fallen into the icy water, too. I wonder if I'll ever get to sleep tonight, Dear Diary.

We keep watch for growlers — a kind of ice that doesn't show up on radar.

Photo by Colin Monteath.

Grandma says this glowing halo is caused by ice crystals in the clouds.

March 10

Dear Diary,

I think what happened yesterday has made me feel even worse today. I can't get the accident out of my mind. There are wonderful icebergs out there today, but I don't feel like going out on deck.

Maybe I'll feel better on my whale watch. On the first day out, I wrote my name on a whale-watching sheet. I watch for whales from ten to eleven every morning. So far I haven't missed a day except for when it was so stormy we weren't allowed on the bridge or outside on the decks!

March 11

Dear Diary,

I just had the thrill of my life! Grandma and I flew in the ship's helicopter! We landed at Cape Hallett, home of the chinstrap penguins. They got their name because of the band of dark fur that goes along the bottom of their face — like a chinstrap.

One of the ship's lecturers is the famous wildlife photographer Colin Monteath. He wanted to photograph chinstrap penguins, and the only way to get to where they are is by helicopter. Colin invited me and Grandma along.

The helicopter was freezing — the same temperature as the air outside! We wore headphones so we could listen to the pilot. It was thrilling to fly above the ice and snow mountains and to see Ross Sea below.

It was exciting to be so close to chinstrap penguins. I got some good pictures.

No one knows why these penguins have chinstrap markings. They just do.

Later

After lunch there was another treat — a party with hot cider on the glacier. But there were more rules! We're not supposed to wander about on the glaciers. There might be *crevasses*, holes hidden by the snow. Mike told me he once fell into a crevasse and broke his ankle. Not me, thank you. This time I obeyed the rules.

Riding the zodiac back to the *Frontier Spirit*, I saw ice drifting toward us! Pack ice! Captain Aye saw it, too. When all passengers were safely on board, he moved the ship to an inlet that was free of ice. That was a close call!

After dinner

The pack ice is chasing us! A huge field of it moved into the inlet where we are. Thank goodness the *Frontier Spirit* could push through it! It was slow going but finally we got out into the clear waters of the Ross Sea.

We had hot cider out on the cold glacier — awesome!

An Adélie penguin takes a bow.

March 12

Dear Diary,

I'm in penguin heaven! Hundreds of Adélie penguins today! ❄ They're so cute — bowing, flopping on their bellies and tobogganing, waddling, running, waving their flipper arms — and pooping. I could smell the penguins from far away. Whew!

I was on the very first zodiac to land on Cape Adare and they practically had to drag me to the last zodiac to take me back to the ship. I didn't want to leave my penguins.

On Cape Adare we visited the hut of the Norwegian explorer Carsten Borchgrevink, built in 1899. His expedition was the first to spend the winter on the Antarctic continent.

When penguins grow a new coat of fur, the old "topcoat" gets loose and falls out. It's called molting. This molting penguin looks scruffy — but cute.

Watch out, Adélie penguins! Here comes your enemy — a leopard seal. ❄

Beside food supplies, I saw socks and shoes. Scientists have been using the hut over the years. Mike found a frozen chocolate bar. Could it be ninety-nine years old?

Someone had written a poem in Norwegian on the ceiling. One of the Norwegian crew translated it:

All the bells chime from far away
All the flowers turn and look back with a sigh.

I think it's beautiful but sad. That explorer-poet, whoever he was, must have missed the sound of music. The only sounds here are the howling winds and the squawking of the penguins, the screeching of the birds, and the belchings of the seals.

The poet must have missed the beautiful flowers that grow in the hills of Norway. What can grow here? ❄

30

Later

There are some days on this trip when one exciting thing piles on top of another. Today is one of those days!

The ship cruised close to a whole army of tabular icebergs. ❄

Then I counted over twenty-four crabeater seals resting on different patches of pack ice. Penguins don't have to be afraid of these seals. Crabeaters feed only on krill — small shrimplike crustaceans. When the ship got really close, the seals stayed right on the ice. Mike says they're scared to get in the water for fear of meeting killer whales, their enemy.

Crabeaters rest on floating ice packs, safe from killer whales.

An ice cave is formed by hundreds of years of pounding ice.

March 13

Dear Diary,

There were no zodiac trips to land today so I spent most of the day in the library, reading about the early explorers.

It's not fair that girls never went on these expeditions. I read a letter sent to the explorer, Sir Ernest Shackleton:

January 11, 1914

We three sporty girls beg of you to take us with you to the South Pole. We are three strong, healthy girls, willing to undergo any hardships that you yourselves undergo. We have been reading books and articles that have been written on dangerous expeditions by brave men to the polar regions. We do not see why men should have all the glory, especially when there are women just as brave and capable.

**I'll miss the ice in all
its wonderful shapes and sizes.**

I agree! When I grow up, I want to be one of the scientists who spends a winter in Antarctica. I'll study penguins or track the weather or study the ozone layer or something else really important. Maybe I'll work for Greenpeace and patrol the sea, protecting the wildlife and preventing pollution.

Bedtime
After dinner, we saw lights from fishing trawlers. They were probably fishing for krill. It's the tiny krill that Antarctic sea life mostly feeds on. If krill was all fished out, the creatures of Antarctica would starve to death. ❄

March 14

Dear Diary,
Here we go again — pitching and rolling on our way north, back to New Zealand. The captain's voice boomed over the intercom: "Don't keep the doctor busy. Hold onto the handrails. We have thirty-foot swells."

I hate to leave Antarctica. Grandma says I've caught ice fever. Penguin fever, too. I'm wondering how I could smuggle a penguin home. There are so many. Would one be missed?

**I wish I could take this
penguin home to be my pet.**

Photo by Dr. Tetsuya Torii.

Later, in the middle of the night

I was fast asleep when the captain's announcement came over the intercom.

"Aurora australis! Wake up everybody! Dress warmly. Come up to deck six."

Sleepily, Grandma and I bundled up. Streams of light streaked across the whole sky. Sometimes the lights were bright, broad ribbons, sometimes pale streamers and fingers. I stayed and watched for three hours, until the night show was finally over. ❄

Now I'm back in my warm bed, writing about it. I'm wondering if it was real or just a beautiful dream. I guess it was real because our clothes are still piled up on the chair and my nose is still cold.

March 17

Dear Diary,

For two days I've been so seasick I couldn't write. Once I even used one of the throw-up bags on the handrails in the corridor.

We had scary gales with thirty-foot-high waves. The ship pitched like anything. Now it was Grandma who felt fine.

The weather is calm again and it's pouring rain. The ship is anchored off Macquarie Island, one of the protected subantarctic islands. The subantarctic islands are completely different from Antarctica. No more icebergs. Or snowy mountains.

I see green hills! Green! I haven't seen green in almost three weeks. And it's Saint Patrick's Day today!

Along the shore there are thousands of penguins. Mike says two hundred thousand king penguins breed here.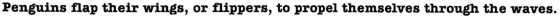

We are not allowed to land on Macquarie, but we'll see the penguins from the zodiacs. I bet I'll be the first to get into the zodiac.

Later

I was the first again! King penguins swam all around us! They seemed as curious about us as we were about them.

Penguins flap their wings, or flippers, to propel themselves through the waves.

The three tanks
are left over
from the terrible
"penguin oil" times.

**The three tanks
are left over
from the terrible
"penguin oil" times.**

On land, thousands of king penguins were packed tight together in a nesting colony. I saw three rusting tanks on the beach. When I found out what they were used for, I almost cried!

It's horrible, Dear Diary. King penguins were led up on ramps and into those tanks. They were boiled down for their oil! That was long ago, after hunters killed practically all the fur seals and elephant seals. I can't stand to think about it!

Giant petrels and skuas were flying back and forth over the huge colony of king penguins. I guess these birds are always on the lookout for penguin eggs or chicks. Mike reminded me again that I shouldn't think badly about these birds. They have to live, too, he said. ❄

The rain was blowing hard in the whipping wind. Some of the passengers wanted to go back to the ship. Not me. I could have watched the penguins for hours.

**A skua is
a dangerous bird
to a penguin.**

Later

For Saint Patrick's Day, the chef baked a green cake in the shape of a shamrock. A lot of the passengers wore green. I was glad I didn't feel seasick green anymore.

After dinner, Captain Aye stopped at our table. He said that the storms on our trip made it his second-worst trip in sixty-two Antarctic expeditions. I asked what was his first worst. "When we were stuck in pack ice for three days," he said. I didn't tell him how scared I've been about pack ice.

The shamrock cake looks too pretty to eat.

Hooker sea lion pups are so adorable.

March 18

Dear Diary,

A lion almost attacked me today! There must have been fifty *sea lions* when I landed on Enderby Island.

I should have waited for Mike or one of the crew to lead the way. But the sea lion pups were just too adorable. I was running up to them when suddenly a huge male sea lion bellowed and charged me. I froze in my tracks, too scared to move. Mike quickly grabbed an oar from the zodiac and got between me and that sea lion. Boy, that was a close call.

Mike said it was good that the biggest sea lion bulls weren't around. A zodiac oar wouldn't have stopped the bulls. He said these are the Hooker sea lions. They're very rare and almost extinct. I hate that word *extinct*. Extinct means gone forever. Never to return.

I'm so lucky, Dear Diary. Mike said that the chances of seeing yellow-eyed penguins are small. These shy penguins hide in the forests. But there they were! They didn't seem to be afraid of me one bit!

Then I climbed a steep muddy hill to where the royal albatrosses were nesting. I fell in the mud. It was worth it, though. I waited in front of one albatross for twenty minutes. I tried not to move so I wouldn't frighten her. At last she rose up to show off her adorable chick.

There were lots of birds on this island. We hiked to a pond where sea lion pups were playing. They weren't afraid of us in the least bit.

Later

Back on the ship, I found a gold-engraved invitation under the door of our cabin. Grandma and I are invited to sit at the captain's table for the farewell dinner!

The royal albatross mother protects her chick.

I told the captain about you, Dear Diary, and he told me about his diary, called a log. Every passenger will get a copy. He asked if he could have a copy of my diary, too. I don't think I'll do it. He'd know about my saying "Aye, Aye, Captain Aye." He'd know what a scaredy-cat I've been about pack ice.

I got very sad at the end of dinner. Tomorrow we'll be landing at the dock in Bluff, New Zealand, right back where we started from. Maybe I'll say, "Bye, bye, Captain Aye."

I'll never forget Antarctica, the last great frozen wilderness on earth. Maybe it's a good thing that the climate is so bitter cold and harsh. It keeps people from living here. And without people to mess it up, maybe it will stay wild and wonderful forever. ❄

And you, Dear Diary, will help me remember everything I learned, everything I felt, and all the amazing things I saw.

Especially the penguins!

More About Antarctica

Here are a lot more facts that Grandma kept for me in her diary.

March 3

Facts About Antarctica, page 6

Antarctica is the fifth largest continent, the size of the United States and Mexico combined. It's one tenth of our world and it's almost completely covered by ice. Ninety percent of the world's ice is here. In some places, the ice is three miles thick. Antarctica is surrounded by the vast Southern Ocean.

In winter, the temperature averages about fifty degrees below zero Fahrenheit. Even in summer, the temperature seldom rises above freezing.

More About Antarctic Winters and Summers, page 7

For more than six months, Antarctica is a cold and lifeless place. Winds of two hundred miles an hour (called *Katabatic* winds) shriek over the frozen seas, and temperatures can fall to one hundred degrees or more below zero Fahrenheit. In mid-winter, it is dark nearly twenty-four hours a day. Only the emperor penguin is here. The other creatures have already traveled north and out to the open sea. During the short summer — November to January — temperatures rise to just about freezing. At the height of midsummer, there are twenty-four hours of daylight. Food is plentiful and this is when most Antarctic creatures breed.

More About the Birds, page 8

Though there are only forty-three species of birds in Antarctica, the total number of birds is

enormous. About seventy-five million sea birds live here. There are tens of millions of penguins. And even more petrels than penguins.

March 4

More About Antarctic Winds, page 10

The middle latitudes nicknamed the Roaring Forties and the Furious Fifties are strong winds that sweep west right around the earth. These nicknames were made up two hundred years ago by sailors who used these westerly winds to sail their ships around the earth.

March 5

More About Ice, page 13

Growlers are small icebergs. Sailors gave them this name because they crunch loudly under the bow of the ship. Ice can float freely or it can be grounded fast. It comes in all shapes and sizes. And when the low afternoon sun sets on ice, it glows golden, lavender, or pink.

March 6

More About the Race to the South Pole, page 15

In October 1911, the English explorer, Robert Falcon Scott, began his race to the South Pole against Roald Amundsen of Norway. They were both trying to be the first person at the South Pole.

Scott's expedition had 16 men, 10 ponies, 233 dogs, and 13 sledges. The ponies were a mistake. It was hard for them to trudge through thick snow. In his tent in a blizzard, Scott wrote, "The weather is steadily sapping the strength of the beasts...." On January 12, Scott wrote, "It is going to be a close run." Four days later, he wrote, "The worst has happened. The Norwegians are first at the Pole. All dreams must go."

During the last two weeks of Amundsen's race to the South Pole, five men and eighteen dogs struggled against thick fog and blizzard after blizzard.

Photo by Colin Monteath.

They were hungry, exhausted, and in pain from frostbite. But on December 14, 1911, he and his fellow explorers put up their flag with "five weather-beaten, frostbitten fists." Amundsen had reached the South Pole just twenty-nine days before Scott.

More About Emperor Penguins, page 16

The female emperor penguin lays a huge single egg right on the ice. Then she leaves for the open sea. For two bitter cold, dark winter months, the male emperor stays on the ice, the egg carefully balanced on his feet. For these eight weeks, the male penguin doesn't eat and he loses half his body weight. The female emperor returns in time for the chick to hatch. Now both parents take turns feeding their hungry chick. Four or five months later, the chick is ready to fend for itself in the sea, though it isn't yet fully grown.

March 8

More About Antarctic Bases, page 19

There are more than fifty bases, most of them along the Antarctica Peninsula. In the winter, the population of all the bases is under one thousand. In the summer, there are more than two thousand. The two largest are the Russian and American bases, where scientists and naturalists work. Naturalists study birds, fish, and mammals. Scientists study weather conditions, volcanic activities, and the hole in the ozone layer.

Ozone is a gas that covers the earth like a blanket. It blocks out sun rays that are too strong for people, plants, and animals. Scientists come to Antarctica to study the thinning ozone layer. They hope to find ways to protect the ozone that protects our earth.

More About Sledge Dog Laws, page 19

Motor toboggans, called "tin dogs," and other machines have replaced the sledge dogs in Antarctica.

The last fourteen dogs from the New Zealand base left in 1987. A law was passed that said seals were no longer allowed to be killed to be used as dog food.

More About Weddell Seals, page 20

On land Weddell seals seem sleepy but in the water they are very active. Weddells dive deep — over two thousand feet! — in search of bottom-dwelling fish. They can stay underwater for over an hour. They cut breathing holes in the sea ice with their teeth.

March 12

More About Adélie Penguins, page 29

For a few weeks each summer the Adélies are very busy. They return to the same place where they were raised. The males get there first and fight for the best nesting spaces. When the females arrive, each finds a mate. They fuss over their nests of pebbles. After the females lay their two eggs, they leave. They cross the ice to feed in the sea. In a month they're back. By then the hungry males have lost half their body weight.

When the tiny, sooty chicks hatch, the parents must protect their chicks from the harsh weather and the skuas, the flying vultures of Antarctica. The parents have to feed themselves as well as their hungry chicks. In a few weeks, the chicks are big enough to be left alone, huddling together for warmth and protection. They begin to molt. Their soft down is replaced with new plumage. Now they are ready to head for the sea.

More About Leopard Seals, page 30

Penguins have reason to fear the leopard seal. This seal usually hunts alone. It waits on pack ice or in icy waters near the penguin rookeries. Then it attacks its prey — a penguin resting on an ice floe or coming home from the sea. Leopard seals also eat fish and squid and they feed on krill. But penguins are their main food.

More About Plants, page 30

Only a few plants can grow in Antarctica and only in the two percent of the continent where there is no ice. The most common are the mosses and lichens. Mosses grow in sandy or gravelly soil and lichens struggle to grow on bare rocks.

More About Icebergs, page 31

Like snowflakes, no two icebergs are the same.

Wind and waves sculpt them into fantastic shapes. Some are tinged green or blue, depending on their age. Tabular icebergs are huge pieces of ice broken off from the ice shelf. Giant bergs eventually break up into thousands of smaller bergs.

More About Krill, page 33

Most Antarctic creatures depend on these small, shrimplike crustaceans. Whales, seals, fish, birds, and squid feed on about 323 million tons of krill every year. Some people want to harvest krill to feed the hungry people of the world. Others worry that krill could be overharvested to the point of extinction.

March 14

More About Aurora Australis, page 34

The beautiful aurora displays are associated with the solar wind, a continuous flow of electrically charged particles from the sun. Sometimes large numbers of these particles reach the earth's magnetic field and cause the upper atmosphere at the two poles to glow. In Antarctica it's called aurora australis. In the north, it's called aurora borealis.

March 17

More About King Penguins, page 35

Like the slightly larger emperor penguins, king penguins don't build nests but hold their single egg on their feet. Unlike the emperors, each king has its nesting territory. They defend their precious area by fighting and squabbling. Penguins fight by batting each other with their flippers and pecking each other with sharp beaks.

More About Skuas, page 36

These birds are known as hawks or vultures of the south. Skuas and giant petrels clean the rookeries of creatures that are weak or sick, dead or dying. Skuas defend their own territories by swooping down on intruders, often hitting them with their tough, leathery webbed feet.

March 18

About the Antarctic Treaty, page 41

Antarctica does not belong to any one country, though many countries would like to own a piece of it. In 1959, an Antarctic Treaty was signed. The countries agreed to let the continent be open to scientists and researchers and to have no military bases there. More than twelve countries have built bases for scientific studies. In 1991, twenty-six members signed an agreement saying there could be no mining or oil exploration for the next fifty years.